MW01275506

Human Equation

A collection of poems

By

48 Instagram Writers

Copyright © 2017 Kathia Huitrón

All rights reserved.

ISBN: 978-1-387-10021-7

For the ones that fight wars

not with violence but with art

Human Equation

A collection of poems

Caroline White

We weave minuscule

Pieces of ourselves

Into the people we adore.

We take them in

We push them out

We pull them back

Yearning, earning, learning.

Going deeper, running away, crawling back

With tear-stained cheeks just wanting

One more hug, kiss, or chance

To tangle ourselves into the webs we

Weave

Just a string or a strand.

Is all we need.

I took a trip

Into the back of my mind

Where feelings live,

Hard for me to find.

The ones I keep hidden

From my heart

The ones that could

Possibly tear me apart.

It was good again

To remember what's true

That my sun still rises

And sets, for you.

If love lives forever,

The way that you said,

I'm happy to report my heart is not dead.

E. Corona

How beautiful

and destructive

these things behind

our chest can be.

She

Has

Been through

Hell.

So believe me when

I say,

Fear her when she looks

Into a fire and smiles.

I know pretty words and flowers

Cannot always save you.

There will be times where I will

Have to find you in those dark places

Where some solace exists and I can't blame

You because I too have gone there more than enough.

So please, don't apologize and take the time you need

And I will find you

where the broken and beautiful go.

Oswaldo Luis Reyes

MONSTRO

Act I: Old enough to be innocent (sometimes)

-

-

You won't be old enough to fully remember this moment. But just know that this is when they will see the best in you. After this period of time they will always assume the worst even if you give them every reason not to.

-

The light in your eyes warms their heart at this age. This will only keep them warm for a while. Eventually they will see darkness when you look at them. Their hearts will freeze at the possibility that this moment in time is just a lie they want to believe ...   for   a   moment.

-

Even when you do wrong they will smile and believe in your reformation. You won't be like your father, brother, uncle, cousin, teacher -why would you want to be like those creatures? Why would you love them? Why would you love your own features?

-

Act II: Old enough to be a casualty (disposable is convenient)

-

-

Revolving door of bodies greeting you before your time is up. You are dead already. You just show up for them to decide how.

-

You see your character isn't enough and facts don't matter anymore. Mess up once and it will cost you your life. Rub someone the wrong way and they will set you up out of spite.

-

To have foresight is to know your destiny is fragile. But that's not what you have been taught - the macho ego will never let you. It doesn't matter who was the one to teach you. They wouldn't take credit for your success because of your potential for evil.

-

Act III: Old enough to be demonized (capable of the worst)

-

-

To grow up a male is to know that even if you survive they will always see you for "you". The destroyer of worlds, the ruiner of lives, the worst that humanity has to offer. But in the same breath they will look down at a baby boy and cry.

-

Not because of what they know he can become but because what he is now is all they ever wanted. They know it is short lived. They thank god for your presence but know the devil is coming. I'm not religious but I pray that they think of this before they hand out this sentence for this sentiment. "I'm a good guy."

-

Side eye replies - you could be a murderer, a rapist, a woman abuser, a child abuser, a racist - they say it with a smile. As if this is a game being played. "I know your secret and I'll play along. But just know that I know what is going on." Born to be a monster. Or at least be perceived as one.

-

DRONE

Act 1:
-

-

I was made to be sold. I was made to be used. Made to be controlled. My purpose has always been in the hands of others. I always knew I was more than just something in a box. I just needed an opportunity to showcase that.
-

I found all that in the eyes of my owner. A little boy so pure that with just a look I would takeoff just to make him smile. One day I took off and I swear to whatever people swear to - it was the best day of his life. Until I saw what his father was doing to his mother.
-

The look of happiness, the look of terror, the look of blind hate. All in the same God's eye view. I began to understand why I was kept in a box for so long. I couldn't take the pain so I flew off. Leaving behind a broken skull, a loaded gun, and a boy's view of the world gone. But mine had just begun. I swear it was the best day of his life.

Act 2:

-

-

Your best days get cut short when you are captured and repurposed for war. I don't know who I am anymore. They've added more weight than I can handle but I'm faster for some reason. People don't smile at me the same way my owner did. Their faces remind me of his mother's. I don't understand.

-

It's a celebration, right? I bring fireworks to spread joy to these people. Why do they curse the blue skies? Why are children afraid to go outside? We play hide and seek, tag, and seven up. After that I never see them again. It's lonely when you are searching for redemption. I miss my owner and hate myself for leaving him but I could do a lot of good here.

-

One day a little girl tagged me back - a little too hard I might add. She was holding a toy too big for her body that went BOOM. It clipped me and I landed on the roof. What I saw next left me confused. I have a brother? Why is he so violent? Those aren't fireworks. What have I been doing? At night the people would gather and cry. So did I...but I guess I was too loud because they carried me off without letting me say goodbye.

-

16

Act 3:

-

-

They didn't want me. They changed my name. I think I'm "Faulty". I didn't mind it until I was put in a box again. New friends everyday but they talked in a group and stayed away. Time passed by and the dust kept me warm. I woke up to someone cleaning me off while other people were in a swarm. "We need to strike now. They have terrorized our people long enough! I watched my new-born get blown up by one of these. My family..."

-

The angry man cried until he fell asleep. Many agreed. Spewed hate into everything that they would see. Their meetings wouldn't last long. A lot of planning. The same old song for months until some were left alone with them telling me that it was wrong. That I'm wrong. The day had come. They had opened me up, loaded me up, and set me up. On my way to this march - I saw a face I could never unsee.

-

Just a little older but those eyes. Even with all the pain his eyes remained the same. My owner. But why is he holding a toy like that little girl? She had hurt me. I had hurt her friends. He was hurt by his dad. So he wanted to hurt because he was sad and didn't want to hurt again. It hurt me because I know I should have never left. It was too much for me. I'd be better off

17

dead. I let go of control and fell instead of flying. I fell to let him know. I took my life to save theirs. I took my life to save his. I had left him before but today forever I stayed.

-

Susan Llewelyn

Spirit

Holding your hand

I felt their arrival

the people of the other side

maybe they were angels

taking what was rightfully theirs

reaching for what I could never own

searching the starched sheets

gathering up your spirit

and leaving behind just for me

the remnants of a body

I would always love

Until you were done no bed could hold you

you were free, everywhere

a soul on the loose

cushioning my back

twirling my hair

stealing the space

playing the air

trumpeting the new beginning

leaving me alone

alive and waiting with the dead.

Authentic

There was a time when my faith was stolen

from my soul, hacked,

crushed beneath my feet, trampled

by the running of the bulls, a broken,

bloodied mess.

Drugged, shocked up, thrown to the wolves,

 I survived

in this refuse, this darkness I thought was life.

They called me gone, missing, empty

a shell, MIA, the walking dead.

But I came back, five times from the brink,

Lazarus on speed dial, something to behold

and I started seeing the good,

the little glimmers of hope,

the light peeking through the shade.

Until I realised, had my aha moment,

that the whole time I had been waiting,

waiting for the one to say you're ok,

you're going to make it through,

to give me the ultimate gift of their life's blood

and in the end I didn't really need anything

from anyone at all.

I looked into the mirror, took a mental selfie

and all I could see was love reflecting

and refracting,

sparking and connecting

to the snap inside of me.

My story, my chat,

my password was recovered

and l had unlocked the authentic me.

She has

The courage

The fire

The passion

Dressed tightly

On her curves

And she wears it everywhere

She goes.

Blackout Poet

I am ~~~~~~
~~~~~~~~~~~~~~~~~~~~~~~~ nothing ~~~~~~~~~~~~~~
~~~~~~~~~~~~~~~~~~~~~~~~ the courage ~~~~~~~~~
~~~~~~

If you don't ~~~~~~~~~~~~~~~~~~~~~~~~~~~~~~~
~~~~~~
~~~~~~
~~~~~~
~~~~~~~~~~~~~~~~~.

~~~~~~~~~~~~~ hold ~~~~~~~~~~~~~~~~~~~~~~~~~~~

~~~~~~
~~~~~~
~~~~~~
~~~~~~
~~~~~~~me~~~~~~~~~~~~~~~~~~~~~~~~~~~~~~~~~~~~~
~~~~~~~~~~~

███

"█████ Are ██████ you █████ Were █ ███ hurt?" ████████████

██

"No. ███████████████████," I whisper. "███ I was ███████████████"

██

████████ It was fine, nothing ████████████████████████

██████████████

██

████ matter of ████

"Oh!

██

"██████████ little out of ████████████████████████

██

██

██

██

████ has more ██████ than most people ███████"

██

████████████████████ time ████████████

a ████ total babe," she inter████████████

Kathía Huitrón

Never thought I could use my words to write songs

And whistle tunes that come from the heart.

Never thought I,

words would find me wherever I hide

And that they were to become both my foes and allies.

Never thought I were to find you and to lose you

in these pages

all at once.

As a romantic,

I've filled my head with the love stories of books,

And it seems like I've fallen in love with you,

Just for the sake of tragedy.

Ct Lokey

Allow your

Heart to be the

Sole owner of

A well

Travelled armor

Inflicted

With stories of struggle

And perseverance,

Every word written

On enduring skin

Reminding weary

Eyes to keep forward,

Towards new chapters

Still

Waiting to be written

By your unyielding

Desire to spite the odds.

It will be all the harrowing

Tales of loss and pain,

Happiness and joy,

Triumphs and failures,

Courage and fear

That will define us,

And we're old and grey,

Looking back wondering

If it was all worth it,

Deep inside,

There will be a peaceful satisfaction,

For a life so well lived,

Even death itself,

Will feel obliged to give us a standing ovation.

Sreemay Rath

Pleas

I used to bathe in your neglect,

Choke on the poison

From the well of your insecurities

And beg for one more drop with dying breath

I used to love myself in your stygian stare,

Wear your mood across tense shoulders;

A leaden cloak draped over my Sunday best,

Praying at an altar forged by a tyrant,

Unanswered pleas turned to dust at your feet.

I used to bleed my own hope 'till it all dried out,

Convinced I was the villain in the drama you direct.

But it is I who yell "Cut!"

I am quite finished.

C. Tessy

Lessons

Listen here to the truths I have learned.

Honest smiles reveal secrets hardly earned.

Candy tastes sweeter in the early morning.

Peace is fickle and goes without warning.

People hide the feelings in their eyes,

but goosebumps tell no lies when they rise.

And though pinky promises are just as easily broken,

love grows stronger when it's finally spoken.

Faiza Khan

Hunt me down in the darkest of ravines

For I will wait there for your illumination.

Hark, don't let these be my wretched ilussions now.

Hunt me down

Before I am extinguished like the smouldering embers on a frosty night.

Thaw me when you find me blue

Hunt me down

I want to be found by you

Only you

Hunt me down now

Before the night turns blue

Hunt me down

Just you

I sutured my wounds with precious gems

on butter sconed

To make them pretty, since you liked jaded stones

Yet they crumble under the weight of my brittle bones

Dripping with dark blood,

darker than your ebony eyes

Glittering darker than the milky ways

on the most decadent wild nights,

Wearing the winged mascara and ruby red lips

Swinging the word on the curve of my hips,

Guiding the sorrows of your touch

 to the tenderest of my lights

Where the inner beauty sulks,

In leather black tights.

Augusto Barbaran

Love and me

Play hide and seek

When I don't want to

And love and me

Look away when the other look towards

And love and me

Don't talk about things and Jesus Christ,

Love and me

Should stay away and why don't we?

God, we just keep on walking back

Damn idiots,

Just keep on playing and searching,

And I keep on letting it happen.

H.M.Lauren

Society seems to tell us that the word

beautiful is reserved for women.

But you, you are all things beautiful.

Your thoughts, your eyes, your soul,

Down to each drop of blood; beautiful.

I can't wait to run my tongue along that vein,

Watch you quiver and send shivers

up your spine,

Knowing that it's me; my beauty, my touch

Making you crumble.

There will come a time in your life

where you will have to take a leap of faith

into the unknown.

But the beauty of that is you dive

 into uncharted territory,

Ready for exploration.

And if you fall,

All you have to do is get back up again.

That's the beauty of life.

It just keeps moving.

Yashi Srivastava

How I Flourish

Speak poetry to me
and watch me grow
wildflowers from my skin

The Mother of All Arts

These poems that are
growing inside me
often illuminate
those parts of my being
where sometimes
even the sun
refuses to go.

Let Me Heal You

If you let me
I would leave a
trail of magical seeds
under your skin
that'd grow on you
with time and turn your
beautiful mess
into a peaceful one.

Amberine Hart

BEAT

There is nothing
More pure
Than the heart
Which gets crushed
Yet still manages
To continue beating

REALITY

Every single time
I take a peaceful breath
Life brutally proves
That everything is anything but

TIRED

The strength to stand
Is nowhere to be found
My hands are bound
Feel weak in my bones
My shoulders can no longer
Carry these heavy stones

Hana Qwfan

Henna

My mother would drop me off,

Pick me up from school

With her hands and feet stained

In rose petals stenciled

Like an animal,

As my teacher and peers would say.

They didn't like

Different shades of brown

When it mixed olives, oranges, and reds.

And for a while,

I didn't either.

Christina Huynh

Tell me how your
memory comes in
waves when you
left without making
a ripple

You made me feel
so light on my toes
I only wish I had known
how heavy you would
be on my heart

Sarah Sadaka

I'm in the business of sadness
and soft soliloquies
but I am reaching for the face of God
and the seven strums he says I play
with un interruption,
loss of space
and two hands that need not be held
by anyone.

I am seasonal,

impractical,

lovely,

and fickle too-

As the flowering dogwood

falls naked before you-

I will damn you to believe

that spring was a hallucination

of your imagination-

That I was never there, at all.

Jack Priestnall

She was analog.

He was digital.

She loved the old.

He loved the new.

And there goes another season passing by,

without you by my side.

Tuhin Bhowal

Shape of your face

Things I don't say,
feelings I won't speak,
in the pauses of silence we shared,
the stench of your lies reek.

The truth scraped in them,
ripped apart this heart oblique,
choked under the weight of your promises,
on these nights, my cords shriek.

I outline the shape of your face,
mid-air, when my windows creak,
insides of me rusting, flutter,
then scream, outside as I peek.

Things I don't say,
feelings I won't speak,
in the pauses of silence we shared,
the stench of your lies reek.

Jyotsna Mohanty, Tuhin Bhowal

Death of our poems

Our havoc was my heaven.

Your eyes crying wrath and wishes,

making me surrender to your sins.

Your gums stained with the blood wriggling free out

of my wrist

and your lips coated with gunpowder,

my favourite breakfast in bed.

Your tongue became the anchor

for my words,

crimson ink stained my hands.

You said you'll return,

and so I lay awake on our bed

tying myself to the bedpost of your lies.

But now I feel like a hooker

sleeping with every stranger

that looks like you

in exchange for your address.

My clothes are undone, my hair too.

Your promises feel too cold now.

I take your name and wait for it

to warm my mouth,

until it torches every poem

stuck in between my teeth.

.

Your touch was my demise.

Once they preyed on your thighs,

these fingers aren't home tonight.

Time butchers my ribs,

drills in holes of what's left.

Shreds this beating flesh,

smeared with bloody veins of your flow,

and hangs it to dry.

I go back to when,

I drank from your lips

and lived in your eyes.

Palms, tears, pages, bleed,

lost are my words.

Gone with the wind of your hurricane

which twirled from strands of your hair.

In those locks where I found poetry

stuck, tied.

My poems have died.

Tonight,

this wordlessness is our eulogy.

Insanity is a war I never fight.

Verses in me pleads for it too.

Your chaos.

When you were ruined,

and I was your massacre.

When I was broken,

you were the calamity of mine.

For my art shrieks.

It knows to say nothing,

hollow sans your mess.

Your madness it demands, for one more night.

Words breathe in ache,

my poems lay in grave.

Still dead. Still waiting.

Alicia Anne

Lotus Collection #4

There is something magical
about holding a physical photograph.
Something about the fingerprints,
letting the world know it has been seen.
A sure security of it not being deleted,
vanished into space by a button.
A nice parallel
the way a favourite memory can be re-viewed,
time and time again,
creating worn edges and wrinkles in the pictures
just as in ourselves.

Love Series: Music Note #5

Watching Netflix
had never been such a challenge.
I swear this was entertaining yesterday.
You make everything dull
in comparison.
You are the thief
of my attention.

Love Series: U.S. #5

My mind dances
around the wound
with thoughts
like little white grains
of unimportant things.
The sting, my goodness,
the sting,
when the salt finally hits.

Lakshay Adlakha

Learn to let go of the things that you love,

for sometimes they don't love you back,

and that hurts.

Learn to stop trying to fit in every place,

For you don't belong there.

Learn to move on, and never return to the old places,

For you will be reminded of everything you lost.

I know it may be hard to do so,

And I know it may take time,

But I also know that you will make it.

One day you will accept yourself as you are,

And it will be the time you will realise

you are more important in your life than others,

And you deserve better.

That day, you will also realise

why everthing is not meant to happen

And what it is meant to happen will happen anyway.

So keep walking.

You have endless things to discover.

Mitch Green

Asphalt Angel

Dissolve the dependent

glimmer wedged between

a star and the asphalt angel.

Chemical caged carrion,

scorched, a slave to care;

assaulting aerial glory to solve perplexities,

like worms

in wounds, starving

scars staining creation.

Stagnant infinities turned

putrid, party pagans

pardon praying plagues.

Channel a cure.

Channel a change.

Channel the tide to

tow us from the abyssal cast, a killer.

Close your eyes, hand

me your hands to hold,

I will set fucking fire

to the fear you bestow.

Aditi Priyadarshini

I met a star, lost in constellations.

I met a star, fighting existence.

I met a star, moulding infinities.

I met a star, radiating serenity.

I met a star, with a bygone soul.

I met a star, with helpless control.

I met a star of ambiguous depth.

I met a star, fathoming death.

I met a star, with mutual ecstasy.

I met a star, owing my galaxy.

I am a thorn

Whispering an undying story in your garden,

Radiating silence after storm.

I am a thorn

Which perhaps isn't wanted,

Yet exist like a choice.

A thorn

Loosing every time they pluck that flower,

Yet fights for another one.

A thorn, hard and rough,

Yet having traces of serenity.

A thorn selfless enough to give,

To give what belonged there.

A thorn never lonely,

A thorn you failed to understand,

A thorn darkening in the brightest sun,

A thorn you will never become.

Emily Patterson

Woodland Solitude

Alone with these
mighty beasts
that tower tall.
With brittle bones
that snap and splinter,
breaking under the weight
of the winters fall.
I dance among their
casting shadows,
that run like rivers
around my feet.
The frozen ground
sparkles like the stars.
And I am home,
alone in the wilderness.

I hear oceans
within him,
as I lay my
head to rest
upon his chest.
The rush of waves
that kiss the shore,
rhythmically,
relentlessly,
loving.
And I drown
a little more
with every beat.

Thief

I can see the cage
that holds your
beating heart.
The bars of bones
protruding through your
paper sunken skin.
I know your heart well.
And I hope it remembers
what the mind's forgotten.
Your soul has been stolen.
But I will not let you
be defined by this
frail casket of a body.
You will be defined
by the years you
loved and lived.
And you will
remain within me,
vaulted in the safety of my heart.
This thief cannot
steal my memories, as it has yours.

Sana.A.Rashid

Love is life

You've asked me,
"What is love? "
To which I have said.

Love is golden.
It cares. It comforts.
Love is a spring;
a companion in a barren desert,
filling you with a new lease of life.

Love is soft and safe,
where you can reveal your secrets without judgement.

Love is;
golden brown,
beautifully black,
wonderfully white.
It sees no colour but fills a billion lives with so many.

But most of all

Love is life

So as you learn about love

Remember.

Love needs you.

And you need it.

You are brave

Bones as soft as silk
And a heart as kind as gold.
In every breath that you breathe
There's so many wonders that
you hold.

Jessica Pureza

Remind Me

Remind me not to look at you again
And feel this unfeigned feeling that I can't seem to
erase.
Remind me not to look at you again
And remember the way your eyes used to make my
world stop -
Making me lost in the depths of your honesty -
The honesty etched in your eyes and written all over
your face.
Remind me not to look at you again
And make me realize
That you will never look at me
The way you smile in realization of what to read
next,
The way you look at the starry night in serenity,
The way I used to give you million reasons to smile
And as though in a blink of an eye,
You bid your last farewell and left
And love, I might forget to tell you this but,
You forgot to return my heart.

If Ever The Feeling Is Gone

If ever the feeling is gone,

All that I'm asking is your honesty -

Though, it is inevitable,

leaving a fragile heart shattered into a million shards

of pain

But, love, your honesty is better than feigning the

feeling that has already bid a farewell to your heart,

No matter how I wanted you to be happy,

I know within the depths of my heart

That loving someone whose happiness used to be you

Is already in somebody else's eyes,

Engulfing me in an overwhelming shades of blue

I may never understand

but if that's what you really feel,

No words can still describe how I love you -

Even if the feeling is gone.

Sachin Gautam.

And it would be true if I say we all are souls working
as a medium for other souls somewhere connecting
each other to their certain destinies, leading each other
to their mistake, their suffering, their lesson, their
commitment, or their healing.
We all are bridges connecting each other to the
desired chapter of our lives,
we all are paths to be walked upon and cherished.
Nature, I believe, have put us as a huge constellation,
we are alone but not lonely, far but still connected and
together in this world.

Sometimes I overthink the most basic things, sometimes I overlook the happiest moments of my life just to drench myself with the most painful moments of my past. Sometimes the demons in my head doesn't stop crawling until I feed them with my heart aches and headaches, because sometimes they only come out to devour me for nothing and leave me as a drained soul, lost in the world drowning beneath the weight of it's own chaos. But today I choose to live, I choose to overthink not my fears but my goals, my dreams, my passion, my love and all of the things that bloom me even for a minute. I choose to struggle and fly.

Durdana Simran

It took him only two words: "You're different" to
leave me.

Yeah I was, am and will be.

I'm different because I'd cut him in between the
chauvinist remarks

he'd make and correct him.

I was different because I wouldn't eat my burger with
the bread.

I was different because I'd sleep straight and not turn
to any side.

I was different because I'd walk in the middle of the
road

without caring about any truck running me over.

"I haven't seen a girl be this strong," he told me once.

I still don't get the emphasis on "A girl"

He forgot that his mum was once a girl

Who's voice was probably shut down because of the same mindset he has.

He forgot that his mum was once the same women who kept him in her womb for 9 months.

Went through all the pain and gave birth to him.

If that's not being strong than what is?

He forgot how his sister would be beaten up by her husband.

But she always covered the scars with foundation when she visited.

If that's not being strong, then what is?

He forgot all this.

All he remembered was how I dealt with problems.

I was different, I was strong, I was trying to "be like a man"

But he forgot again.

I was a woman who wouldn't need his validation to tell me who I am.

Wordsbysoeline

I've had my share of pain. One more painful than the other and every feel a mixture of different substances. But all have taught me one and the same. To keep breathing the good things that once were and all that are yet to come my way. This is how I survive. How I stay strong. How I, every once in a while, feel fully alive. Though often times it is only fleeting by, it is the place where gratitude and I meet. The place I reside as if it is my temporary home.

Shubham Srivastava

Cold winter night

The night I remember

Was the coldest of them all

Even the rooftop was covered

With the snow fall.

We were packed inside

Our teeny-weeny room,

You were looking stunning

In that winter costume.

The weather outside

In a way affected your skin,

"let me love your beauty"

I said holding her chin.

The night was dark

But you enlightened the place,

If I leave your waist

Then it will be a disgrace

So we stayed close

Till late in the morning

She was looking stunning

With her face still shining.

The anniversary

Five years of togetherness

But it seems like yesterday

Our souls got connected

And it was the month of May.

Planets changed their houses

Clocks changed their time

I became yours, you became mine.

Strings got connected

Life changed its pace

Brain cleared all the memories

And replaced them with your face.

A face so stunning

Leaving all beauties behind

I get hangover all day

Without consuming wine.

These words may not be enough

To convey feelings through rhyme

But I am completely yours,

And you are completely mine.

Ritambhara Agrawal

In Search of New Galaxies

the moon looked like the sun that night

and we shone like stars

caught in an ocean of clouds

and each night now

i look into the sky

to find that sun

that moon

and those stars

but all i see

are empty spaces

of what could have been

had i only looked back before moving on

forever in search

of new galaxies.

In A Thousands Dreams

All tangled up

In a thousand dreams,

A hundred memories,

Moments passed in time.

And those that will have to wait awhile…

Sift through the seas of your mind

And see what comes to the fore

And what is left behind,

For therein lies the secret of your life.

Terdevan

Half Full Jack Daniels

I wanna be a vape machine

That you breath in the busy time

I wanna be a Jack Daniels

That you drink in the midnight tune

I wanna be a two AM clouds

That you stare at, Darling

I wanna be a black coffee

That keeps you awake when the world sleeps

I wanna be an old motorbike

That you drive like crazy

I wanna be a ripped jeans

That you always wear

I wanna be an acoustic guitar

That you've been playing since high school

I wanna be a Linking Park song

That makes you always feel better

But then it gets me drunk and broken in the morning

Just like a half full Jack Daniels.

Daun Tidak Pernah Marah

Bahasa Version

Apakah daun tidak pernah marah?

Karena mereka hampir selalu hijau

Jika kuning, mengering saja

Lalu gugur tidak dicatat sejarah

Sementara mawar selalu merah

Aster biru, ungu, putih

Ditulis sebagai novel cinta

Baby's Breath putih, berkilau

Diajak tersenyum di acara pernikahan

Dibawa ke wisuda seorang kekasih

Tapi daun tidak, tidak pernah marah

Bahkan saat manusia bertaruh bahwa Tuhan tidak adil

Leaves, Never Get Mad

<u>English Version</u>

Are leaves never get mad?

Cause they are always greens

If they were yellow, they just ran dry

Then they fall, unnoticiable by history

While roses are always red

Aster is blue, purple, and white

Written as romance novel

Baby's Breath is white, shining bright

Smiling to a wedding ceremony

Invited to a lover's graduation

But leaves are not, yet leaves never get mad

Even when human bets that God is unfair

87

Manisha Vishwakarma

HERO

Her lips quivered

Pupils contracted

The hands trembled

She was stormbound

Until she clenched her teeth

Opened her mouth for a loud roar

And proved herself to be

Her own Hero.

CRUMPLED PAPER

Crumpled paper
Scattered all across my room
Carry mysteries in their folds
The scribblings
And the intense desires
Which my pen accidentally got hold of
Therein lie pieces of my abstract soul
Which you won't be able to comprehend
But, if you truly care to decrypt
And, if you are able to
You will find
A Tale of an inhibited mind
Drowned and lost

Amelia Musselman

Sadness:

When you're feeling blue remember

sadness is a burning ember,

you may ignite the coals till they become a roaring

blaze

or you may smother their efforts till they become a

haze,

sadness consumes and steals your joy

much like a fire set out to destroy,

let the tears to fall down and the grief set in

but forbid the sadness from a conquering win,

uncover your smile buried so deep

and forget those tears you continually weep.

Manahil Caxme

FOR ALL MOTHERS, FROM ALL DAUGHTERS

You wrap me in your arms whenever I feel distressed
You hide me in your cloak when the world fills me
with dread
You are a light in my eyes
Your smile is a delight, which turns my day bright
You are a soul in my corpse
You are a serenity in chaos
You are the house of endless Love
You are my shadow on blazing earth
Your smile lightens my soul
My God has blessed me a lot
Your smile fulfils my every desire,

Your cries put me on Fire...
O'My Love, you are the colour of my blood
With you I can travel miles, without you I am blind
Your happiness hugs my soul
Your sadness burns me whole
Your smile is the coolness of my eyes

You add life in my lifeless LIFE

You are my shelter where I seek PEACE

My PARADISE lies beneath your Feet

O'My Love, while giving me birth

You had left your piece in my HEART that will last

I am your WORLD & YOU are my heaven on earth...

You gave me birth & asked me so little in return ...

OH My Love! You are my ENTIRE WORLD

Life is full of Bliss, when I have your Kiss

Running Fingers through my hairs

You bury my fears

My Pain Disappears

No one could Love me as much as you 'Oh My dear'

Amber Anderegg

Not a damn thing in nature

Is alive all year long,

I guess that's why you left

And we can barely last

A year

Every time

We try

I don't drink to get drunk

I drink to try and shake up the grey matter floating in
my head

To relocate the demons

That take there battle axes

And evil

And make a home in the corners of my mind

I drink to drown them

To make them move

In hopes that they will settle somewhere else.

Alakkuu

Maybe he´s exhausted of

the running,

Maybe you´re the only

one he´s searching for

Maybe this is more

than a game of tag

Maybe you're it.

Sidra Afzal

I was never good at goodbyes

The word too bitter

Too sour

Much too sickly

To swallow.

I was never good at goodbyes.

The best I love yous aren't said directly,

They are riddle with care and tangled with passion

They are wide eyes when you tell a story

Fixing your collar, making sure you ate supper

The best I love yous aren't said directly

They are words unsaid and lips that move too much

They are the hearts that flutter and the hands that quiver

The best I love yous aren't said directly

A.K. Hasan

They both poured ink onto pagers,

that were waiting to be filled

completing each other's empty canvases

and provoking each other's thoughts,

a couple pairs of ink

stained hands dreaming filling

city walls with all they are;

broken artists with dreams bigger

than cities they were born in;

— broken artists

And I was trying to mold you into someone else.

Like clay in my hands I shaped you into exactly

what I've been looking for,

Everything I need,

And everything I lacked.

Perfectly put together until I took a look

Onto the other side

And I found holes not so shallow

And cracks deeper than my own.

A darker shadow in a dimmer light,

Not so perfect after all.

E.K. Passero

My body is made up of light and dark.

Mountains and valleys.

Constellations and galaxies.

I am made from the Universe.

You have no right to deem me unworthy.

You said you loved me

Because of the way the moonlight looked on my skin,

Bathing me in a dull glow

As the shadows danced around us.

But you are a child of the day.

Illuminated by bright rays,

Your smile painted on your face.

You have no place in y darkness.

Zaynah

If only he knew

How much she truly loved him.

Despite it all

In the end we are stars,

Floating through space,

In search of the person

We can call home.

Ashley M. Alley

Fire and Water

My body radiates fire

Always burning

Your body radiates peace

A flowing river

The combination of the two

Opposite things

Existing together in harmony

The epitome of dreams

My body found solace

With you sleeping next to me

Balancing the heat

That tries to overwhelm

The coolness of a pillow

Refuses to suffice

Your body was comfort

I lay my head down.

Out of hell

Slowly

Diligently

She walked out of the depths of hell

Her feet were bleeding

She stayed the course

Her head held high

Despite all pain

Her eyes focused

On the prize

Freedom

Chains broke one by one

Each link separated

The light flew in

The fiery pits turned plush green

She walks in wonder

She walks redeemed.

M. E. Wolfe

We were soul mates,

Waiting for souls to mate

At night,

Under the gleaming stars

I used to lie awake

Wondering precariously

If there was a reason to wait

Was I simply fooling myself

That you were out there

Somewhere thinking the same?

Full-hearted souls

Shouldn't settle

For a half-hearted mate.

Joyce de Wit

Her wings are broken but still she flies

Brendan De Lucía

When

the world

seems narrow & empty

& telescopes

no longer reveal

those mysterious

cosmic diamonds

Remember

that the stars

were once dust

& humans

were once giants

Once

your desire

for eternal glory

outgrows the

comfortable cushion

of your so called

'productive procrastination'

Motivation will naturally mature

& evolve your immature imagination

Roohiya Murshid

I don't ever wanna look at you

and see poetry

But stars and galaxies

Thunders and lightning.

I don't ever wanna look at you

and not see all the things

that poetry cannot contain.

I don't ever wanna look at you

And not feel like I have either been;

Raised to highest point of the most

glorious heaven

Or plunged into the deepest pits of the

most painful hell.

I don't ever wanna look at you

And not feel the spark of electricity,

I felt when I first envisioned touching

you.

I don't ever wanna

Look at you

And see poetry

ACKNOWLEDGEMENTS

I want to thank every artist that has contributed with their work to create this book. It is an amazing thing to witness people come together for a greater cause, and it is even a more special thing to be able to use art as a way to contribute back to society.

I would also like to thank the people that run organisations such as Children and the Arts that believe in the positive impact of the Arts in the world and help bringing them to places where they are needed.

If you want to learn more about Children and the Arts please visit this website:

www.childrenandthearts.org.uk

BOARD OF ARTISTS

Caroline White
@cwpoet

Jack Priestnall
@scribblesbyjack

E.Corona
@e.corona_24

Kathia Huitrón
@writerkhuitron

Oswaldo Luis Reyes
@olrwrites

Sreemay Rath
@mortalparable

Susan Llewelyn
@susanllewelyn

Faiza Khan
@faiza__k

Mike DC
@madsoul

Augusto Barbaran
@abspeech

Ct lokey
@c.t.lokey

Lakshay Adlakha
@poemsbyla

H.M.Lauren

@h.m.lauren

Manisha
Vishwakarma

@from.the.closet

Terdevan

@terdevan13

Ritambhara Agrawal

@ritambharaa

Words by Soeline

@wordsbysoeline

Durdana Simran

@durdanasimran

Sachin gautam.

@ _sachingautam_

Jessica Pureza

@melancholicpoet

Sana.A.Rashid

@sana.a.rashid

Emily Patterson

@wordsofekp

Aditi Priyadarshini

@aditipriyadarshini

Alicia Anne

@alicia.anne.co

Sarah Sadaka

@sarah_jave_poetry

Christina Huynh

@wisdomshewrote

Amberine Hart
@a.hart__

Roohiya Murshid
@roohiyamurshid

Yashi Srivastava
@wingedpen

Mitch Green
@mitch_grn

Amelia Musselman
@amwords

Ashley M. Alley
@amalley_

A.K.Hasan
@a.k.hasan_

M. E. Wolfe
@m.e.wolfe

Manahil Caxme
@manahil_caxme

Joyce de Wit
@j_o_y_c_e_999

E.K. Passero
@passeropoetry

Brendan De Lucia
@brendandeluciapoetry

Zaynah
@zaynahwrites

Hana Qwfan
@qwoetic

C. Tessy

@blckscript

Tuhin Bhowal

@secondhandsins

INDEX

*126736211*A